Games & Pu

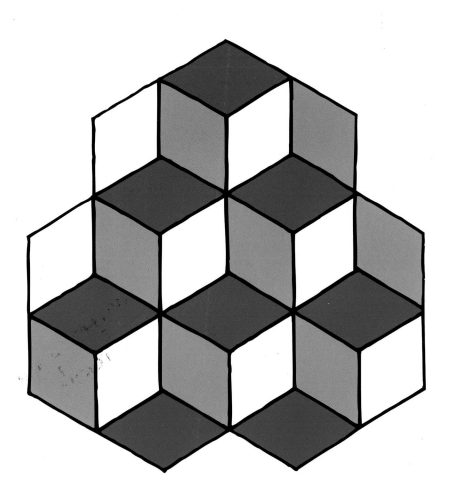

David Kirkby

Heinemann

First published in Great Britain by Heinemann Library
an imprint of Heinemann Publishers (Oxford) Ltd
Halley Court, Jordan Hill, Oxford OX2 8EJ

MADRID ATHENS PARIS
FLORENCE PRAGUE WARSAW
PORTSMOUTH NH CHICAGO SAO PAULO
SINGAPORE TOKYO MELBOURNE AUCKLAND
IBADAN GABORONE JOHANNESBURG

Designed by The Point
Cover design by Pinpoint Design
Printed in China
Produced by Mandarin Offset
99 98 97 96 95
10 9 8 7 6 5 4 3 2 1

ISBN 0431 06901 8

British Library Cataloguing in Publication Data
Kirkby, David
Games. - (Maths Live Series)
I. Title II. Series
793.74

Acknowledgements
The author and publisher wish to acknowledge, with thanks,
the following photographic sources:

Skyscan Balloon Photography p18; 1995 MC Escher/Cordon Art Baarn
Holland; Trevor Clifford p40.
The publishers would also like to thank the following for the kind loan
of equipment: NES Arnold Ltd; Polydron International Ltd.

Note to reader; words in **bold** in the text are explained in the glossary on page 44.

CONTENTS

1 DOMINOES

Dominoes are used for many different games and puzzles. A full set contains 28 dominoes, ranging from a double blank to a double six. In many domino games you have to join one domino to another domino on the table, so that they meet with a matching number of spots.

It is possible to make a chain of dominoes using all 28, so that they meet with matching numbers of spots. It is also possible to make matching shapes. Below are two different domino squares.

DOMINO RECTANGLES

Using a set of dominoes, can you make domino rectangles, meeting with matching numbers of spots, to fit these arrangements?

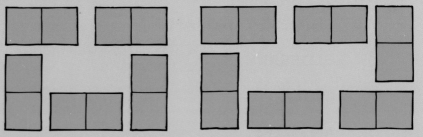

If the dominoes with a blank are removed, and the others are sorted into columns according to their total numbers of spots, then a **symmetrical pattern** is created. This shows that there are three dominoes which have a total of six spots, of seven spots and of eight spots.

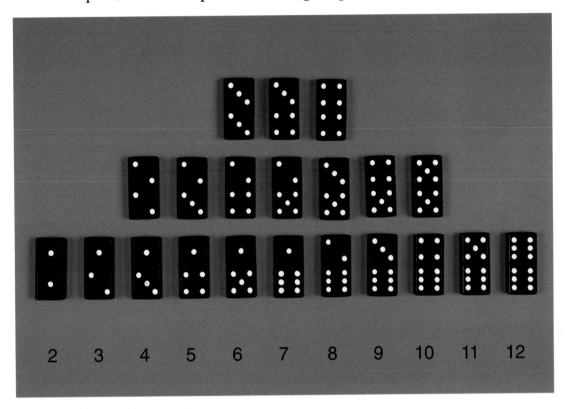

DOMINO ADDITIONS

It is possible to arrange three dominoes to make addition sums like the one shown.

Can you make some more?

$$62$$
$$+\ 2$$
$$\overline{}$$
$$64$$

5

2 COINS

Many puzzles use coins. One reason is that they are easy to slide, although in some cases counters can be used as a replacement. Another reason is that each face is different (head or tail).

COIN ILLUSION

Try this illusion with coins to test your skills of observation. Place three coins in a row. Slide the middle coin until you think that the distances x and y are the same. Then use a ruler to see if you are correct.

FLIPPING COINS

Start by placing nine coins like this, so that there are eight heads and one tail. A move consists of turning over all three coins in any row, column or **diagonal**. Can you finish with all nine coins head-up? It can be done in 5 moves.

COIN SWAP

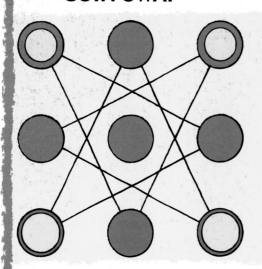

Place two small and two large coins like this. Slide a coin along a line to an empty spot. Can you swap the positions of the small and large coins? How many moves does it take?

Other coin puzzles use the value of the coins themselves.

COIN SHARING

In this puzzle you need the coins shown here.

The money must be shared equally between two people.
Can you find three different ways of sharing the money?

COIN GAME

This is a game for two players to practise skills of addition. You need one coin. The first player places the coin on any spot and says the number. The second player slides the coin along a line to another spot, and says the running total by adding on the new number on the spot. Continue taking turns to slide the coin and say the running total. The first player to say a total which is more than 30 loses.

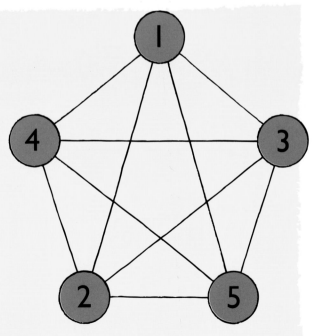

③ STRAWS

There are many different types of straw puzzles. Many involve making shapes.

STRAW SQUARES

Make this shape with short straws.
- Remove 2 straws to leave 5 squares.
- Remove 3 straws to leave 4 squares.
- Remove 4 straws to leave 3 squares.
- Remove 4 straws to leave 4 squares.
- Remove 5 straws to leave 4 squares.

STRAW DIVISION

This type of puzzle is based on adding more straws. Make this shape with short straws. Add 8 more short straws so that the shape can be divided into four equal parts.

STRAW EQUATIONS

These puzzles use short straws to make Roman numerals.

Make these equations with straws. In each case move one straw to a new position to make each equation correct.

NIM

This is a game for two players.
- Take a handful of straws and make two piles.
- Take turns to remove any number of straws from one pile.
- The winner is the player who takes the last straw.

4 CARDS

There are hundreds of different games, tricks and puzzles based on a pack of playing cards.

DOUBLES

Start by removing the picture cards. The aces represent the digit 1. The idea is to make pairs of numbers so that one number is double the other.

Here are some examples.

Find your own set of playing cards and see how many 'doubles' you can make.
How many 'trebles' can you make?

TRIPLETS

Use the ace to ten of spades only.
Find a set of three cards which total 12: for example, 2, 3 and 7.
It is possible to find seven different triplets altogether.
Can you find them?

There are ten different triplets which have a total of 15.
Can you find them?
You must make sure that they are all different!

GUESS MY CARD

This is a game for two players.
- Player A chooses a card, looks at it, then hides it.
- Player B has to guess what the card is by asking a series of questions.
- A may only answer 'Yes' or 'No'.
- Count how many questions are needed before the card is guessed correctly. The winner is the player who needed fewer guesses. Swap roles, so that B has to guess A's card.

SIXTEEN CARD PUZZLE

This is a card puzzle which seems easy to start with, but then becomes more and more difficult.

You need to take the four aces, the four twos, the four threes and the four fours from the pack. The sixteen cards have to be arranged in a 4 x 4 pattern.
- Can you arrange the cards so that the same number does not appear in any row?
- Now can you arrange them so that the same number does not appear in any row or column?
- Lastly, can you arrange them so that the same number does not appear in any row, column or diagonal?

5 DICE

Dice have been used in games for hundreds of years. This is because, when they are rolled, each face has an equal chance of facing upwards, and so winning or losing depends on chance. The most common type of dice is a cube with spots on each of the six faces, but all sorts of different dice are available.

MAKE A SIX-FACED DICE

You need some thin card.
- Use a ruler to draw this net of six squares.
- The edges of the squares should be 6 cm.
- Add tabs, cut it out, and crease along the lines.
- Draw the spots on the squares.
- Fold it and glue the tabs to make your dice.

MISSING SPOTS

The opposite faces of a spotty six-faced dice always total 7. These are nets of dice with spots missing from some of the faces. Can you work out how many spots there should be on each missing face?

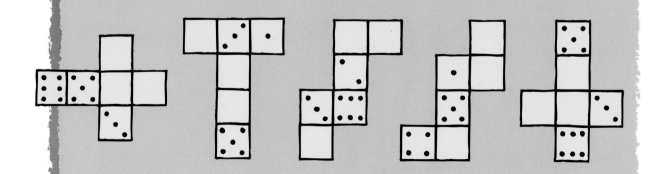

IMPOSSIBLE DICE

Some of these drawings are different views of the same dice. Some are impossible. Which are the impossible dice? Use a dice to help you.

1 TO 20

Throw three dice.

Then see how many of the numbers 1 to 20 you can make using the three numbers on your dice. Each dice number can only be used once each time. But you don't have to use all three numbers. Here are the answers using 1, 4, 5.

(1) = 5 - 4	(6) = 5 + 1	(11) = 15 - 4	(16) = (5 - 1) x 4
(2) = 5 + 1 - 4	(7) =	(12) =	(17) =
(3) = 4 - 1	(8) = 5 + 4 - 1	(13) =	(18) =
(4) = 5 - 1	(9) = 5 + 4	(14) =	(19) = 15 + 4
(5) = 4 + 1	(10) = 5 + 4 + 1	(15) = (4 - 1) x 5	(20) = 4 x 5

6 DICE GAMES

There are many different types of games with dice.
These pages show some examples which require number
skills. In the first game, you need to be able to keep a
running total of your score as you throw the dice.

THREE LIVES

This is a game for two or more players.
You need one dice. On your turn you continue throwing
the dice, keeping a running total of your score. Each time
you throw a '1' you lose a 'life'. When you have lost three
'lives', your turn ends and you record your score. The
winner of the round is the player with the highest total.

NUMBER STRIPS

This is a game for two players.
You need at least four dice. On your turn throw as many
dice at once, as you like. Find their total, and place a
counter on the same number on the board. If this is not
possible, or the number is already covered by a counter,
then do nothing. The winner is the first player to get
either 5 counters in any one strip, *or* 4 counters on each of
two strips.

1	2	3	4	5	6
7	8	9	10	11	12
13	14	15	16	17	18
19	20	21	22	23	24

FIVE HOME

This is a dice game for one person.
You need one dice and five counters. Place one counter on each of the five starting spots.

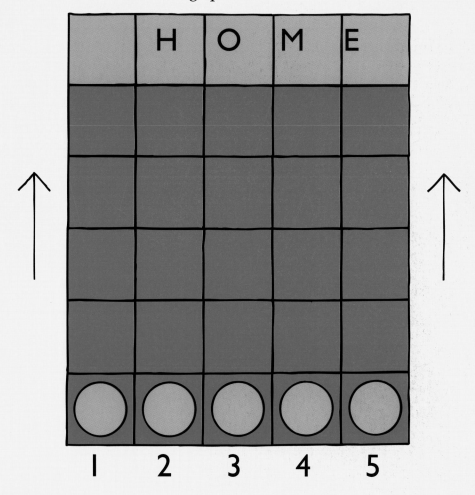

Throw the dice and move counters to match the dice number. For example, if you throw a '5' then you can move:
• the 5-counter one space forward
• or the 1-counter five spaces forward
• or the 4-counter and 1-counter each one space forward
• or the 3-counter and 2-counter each one space forward.
Each time you throw the dice, make a tally mark on a sheet of paper, to record how many throws you have had.
Can you get all the counters 'home' in fewer than 25 throws?

BOARD GAMES

It is easy to make a board like the one on the opposite page. Use it to play different games. These games are all for two players.

You need a set of counters each of your own colour.

SUM AND DIFFERENCE

You need two dice.
Take turns to throw both dice and place a counter on a number on the board to match: *either* the sum of the two dice numbers *or* the difference between the two dice numbers. If you cannot place a counter, do nothing. The winner is the first player to have four counters in any one straight line (horizontal, vertical or diagonal).

MULTIPLICATION

You need a pack of playing cards with the picture cards removed. Shuffle them and place them face-down in a pile. Take turns to pick up the top two cards and multiply the card numbers together. Place a counter on a number which matches the units digits of the answer.

For example, if the cards are 7 and 4, multiply them to make 28, and place a counter on 8. The winner is the first player to have three counters in any one straight line.

SUBTRACTION

You need two dice.
Take turns to throw either one or two dice. If you throw two dice, find the total. Subtract your dice score from 12, then place a counter on a matching number. When all the numbers have been covered, the winner is the player who has placed the most counters.

2	5	4	8	9
0	3	6	2	5
8	6	1	7	4
9	5	0	8	3
1	7	4	6	7

TO DO:

Make your own board, by writing numbers in a grid.
Invent some rules for a game and play it.

8 MAZES

One of the best-known mazes is at Hampton Court Palace near London. The maze is built with high hedges.

MAZE CHALLENGE

Can you find the quickest way through the maze?

MAKE YOUR OWN MAZE

Start with an 8 x 8 square grid.
1 Place the hidden treasure in one of the squares. Draw a route from the treasure to the outside (the entrance).
2 Draw some fences.
3 Then copy the drawing again, without showing the route.

1   2   3

NUMBER MAZE

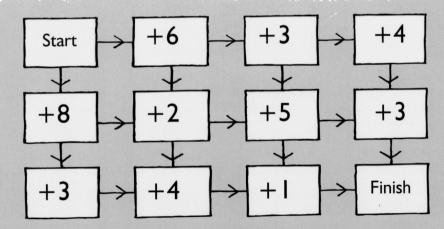

Find a pathway from Start to Finish. You must follow the direction of the arrows.
- Can you find a pathway which totals 15?
- Which pathway gives the largest total? Which pathway is the smallest total?
- How many different totals are possible?

9 TARGETS

Many sports and games are based on aiming at a target and scoring points.

TARGET TOTALS

Look at these three targets.
Suppose you can have three shots at each target.
What is the largest possible total score for each target?

What are all the different possible scores with three shots at target number 1? How many different scores are possible for targets 2 and 3?

TO DO:

Invent your own target and points for each ring.
Investigate all the different possible scores with three shots.

Another well-known target game is darts.

A Darts which are thrown into the outer
ring of the board count double the score.
B Darts in the inner ring count treble the score.
C Darts in the inner bullseye count 50 points.
D Darts in the outer bullseye count 25 points.

There are many different variations of
the game of darts. In most of these,
players are allowed to throw three
darts at each turn.

*What score is made with the darts in
the photograph?*

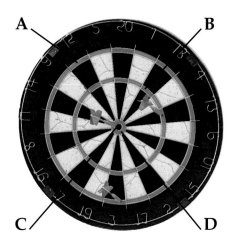

DICE DARTS

This is a game for two or more players.
You need one dice numbered 1 to 6.
Make another dice by writing S, S, D, D, T, T on the faces
of a cube (S stands for 'single', D for 'double' and T for
'treble').
Take turns to throw both dice, and find your score.
If you throw   for example,

then your score is treble 4: 12.
Play ten rounds each, keeping score on a scoresheet.
The winner is the player with the largest total score.

VARIATION

Now write 5, 6, 7, 8, 9, 10 on the faces of another cube,
and use this instead of the dice numbered 1 to 6.

NUMBER TRICKS

Here are some number tricks to amaze your friends. They are devised so that they always produce the same answer. The first trick, for example, always gives the answer 6.

ANSWER 6

Start by secretly writing a large number 6 on a piece of paper or card, then placing it in an envelope and sealing it. Give the sealed envelope to a friend.

Then ask your friend to:
- write down any number
- double it
- add 20
- subtract 8
- divide by 2
- subtract your original number
- open the envelope!

Here are two more envelope tricks to try.

ANSWER 23

Seal the number 23 in an envelope. Tell your friend to:
- write down any three-digit number
- add 25
- multiply by 2
- subtract 4
- divide by 2
- subtract your original number
- open the envelope!

ANSWER 3

Seal the number 3 in an envelope. Tell your friend to:
- write down any number
- treble it
- add 12
- double it
- subtract 6
- divide by 2
- divide by 3
- subtract your original number
- open the envelope!

Try this trick with three dice on a friend.

ADD 7

Ask a friend to throw the three dice, unseen by you.
Tell your friend to:
• find the total
• turn one of the dice upside down and add the number on the bottom
• roll this dice again and add whatever number appears
• write down the total score in secret.
You can now look at the three dice and say what the total is.

Secret

Add seven to the total of the three dice you can see.

Here are two more dice tricks to try.

SUBTRACT 150

Ask a friend to throw three dice, unseen by you.
Tell your friend to:
• double the number on the first dice
• add 3
• multiply by 5
• add the second dice number
• multiply by 10
• add the third dice number
• tell you the result.
You can now say the scores on the three dice.

Secret

Subtract 150 from the result.

SUBTRACT 110

Ask a friend to throw three dice, unseen by you.
Tell your friend to:
• multiply the number on the first dice by 10
• add 11
• add the second dice number
• multiply by 5
• double it
• add the third dice number
• tell you the result.
You can now say the scores on the three dice.

Secret

Subtract 110 from the result.

The digits of your answer are the numbers on the dice!

11 AGE TRICKS

Here are some tricks to help you find out someone's age.
Try them out on yourself first.

AGE TRICK 1

Ask someone to:

- write down any three-digit number
- rearrange the digits to make another three-digit number
- subtract the smaller number from the larger
- add your age (say, 10)
- tell you the answer.

You can now tell them their age.

$$
\begin{array}{r}
613 \\
-136 \\
\hline
477 \\
+10 \\
\hline
487
\end{array}
$$

Secret

Add the digits of the answer until you have a single-digit number, i.e. $4 + 8 + 7 = 19$, then $1 + 9 = 10$ and $1 + 0 = 1$.
Add this number to a **multiple** of 9 which gives an approximate age: $1 + 9 = 10$.

AGE TRICK 2

Ask someone to:

- write down their house or flat number   71
- double it $71 \times 2 = 142$
- add the number of days in a week $142 + 7 = 149$
- multiply by 50 $149 \times 50 = 7450$
- add their age (say, 11) $7450 + 11 = 7461$
- subtract the number of days in a year (365) $7461 - 365 = 7096$
- add 15. $7096 + 15 = 7111$

house number ⌐ age

You can work out their house number and age from the answer.

AGE TRICK 3

Ask someone to look at the table and say which columns their age appears in. Then add together the top numbers in each of these columns to find their age.

For example, if they say their age is in the first, third and fifth columns, then you add together 1, 4 and 16 to give their age of 21.

1	2	4	8	16	32
3	3	5	9	17	33
5	6	6	10	18	34
7	7	7	11	19	35
9	10	12	12	20	36
11	11	13	13	21	37
13	14	14	14	22	38
15	15	15	15	23	39
17	18	20	24	24	40
19	19	21	25	25	41
21	22	22	26	26	42
23	23	23	27	27	43
25	26	28	28	28	44
27	27	29	29	29	45
29	30	30	30	30	46
31	31	31	31	31	47
33	34	36	40	48	48
35	35	37	41	49	49
37	38	38	42	50	50
39	39	39	43	51	51
41	42	44	44	52	52
43	43	45	45	53	53
45	46	46	46	54	54
47	47	47	47	55	55
49	50	52	56	56	56
51	51	53	57	57	57
53	54	54	58	58	58
55	55	55	59	59	59
57	58	60	60	60	60
59	59	61	61	61	61
61	62	62	62	62	62
63	63	63	63	63	63

There are interesting patterns of numbers in some dates.

CENTURY DATES

1st March 1996 is a century date
    1 – 3 – 96
because 1 + 3 + 96 = 100.
Find some more century dates.

CONSECUTIVE DATES

10th September 1987 is a consecutive date
    10 – 9 – 87
so is 6th July 1989
    6 – 7 – 89
Why is 31st March 1993 a strange date?
Can you find more like it?

PALINDROMES

A palindrome reads the same forwards as backwards.
Here are some examples of palindromic words.

level	gag	rotator
deed	noon	civic
did	pip	radar

Palindromic Party Guest list

Mum   Bob

Dad   Lil

Anna   Hannah

Some names are palindromic. *Who else could we invite to the party?*

Some people have spent a long time trying to create palindromic sentences. Here are some examples:

Madam, I'm Adam.
Norma is as selfless as I am, Ron.
Doc note, I dissent, a fast never prevents a fatness, I diet on cod.

Palindromic numbers can be of different sizes.
Here are some palindromic three-digit numbers.

THREE-DIGIT PALINDROMES

There are another 27 palindromic numbers between 100 and 400.
Can you find them?

171
222
363

If we start with any two-digit
number, say   26
Reverse the digits and add: $26 + 62 = 88$
                              (a palindrome in 1 step)

Now let's try with 57   57
Reverse the digits and add: $57 + 75 = 132$
Reverse these digits and add: $132 + 231 = 363$
                              (a palindrome in 2 steps)

TWO-DIGIT PALINDROMES

Try this with your own two-digit numbers.
Do all two-digit numbers become palindromes?

PALINDROMIC TIMES

The clock time is palindromic.
Find some more palindromic
times.

PALINDROMIC DATES

Some dates are palindromic.
What is the next palindromic date?
1991 was the last palindromic year. Which is the next?

13 OPTICAL ILLUSIONS

An optical illusion is a picture or drawing which seems to play tricks on your eyes.

Study this picture. Is there anything wrong with it?

These drawings will test your eyes.

*Which **horizontal line** is longer, A or B?*

*Which of the two **vertical lines** is longer, C or D?*

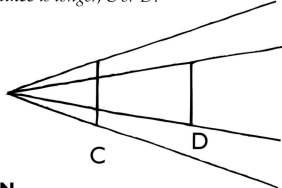

DRAW AN ILLUSION

Draw two straight lines which are the same length, and label them A and B.

Draw some more lines to try to make A and B appear to be of different lengths.

Ask a friend to judge which is the longer.

COUNTING CUBES

Look carefully at this picture, until you can see some cubes. Count them.

Keep looking until you can see a different set of cubes, and count these.

It is possible to count one set of six cubes and one set of seven cubes.

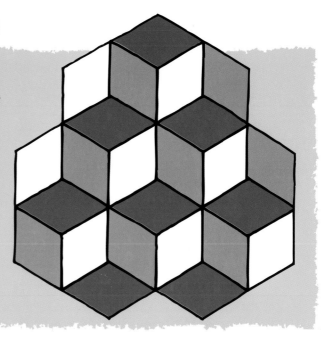

Escher, a Dutch artist, created many pictures which contained optical illusions. This one, called *Belvedere*, was drawn in 1958.

Study it carefully, and pay particular attention to the ladder.

MAGIC SQUARES

A **magic square** is a square grid containing a different number in each square of the grid. It is called 'magic' when all of its rows, columns and diagonals have the same total.

Check that this is a magic square. The total of each row, column and diagonal is 15.

Its **magic number** is 15.

4	9	2
3	5	7
8	1	6

MAGIC SQUARES

Here are some more magic 3 x 3 squares. What is the magic number in each case?

3	10	5
8	6	4
7	2	9

5	12	7
10	8	6
9	4	11

4	11	6
9	7	5
8	3	10

NON-MAGIC SQUARES

Make nine cards numbered from 1 to 9, and place them in a 3 x 3 square grid. Can you arrange them so that all the rows, columns and diagonals have different totals?

Albrecht Dürer, a German artist, created this 4 x 4 magic square in 1514. Check that its rows, columns and diagonals all total 34. This square is extra special because the magic number of 34 appears in the total of the numbers in all four corners, the four central squares, and each of the four corner 2 x 2 squares.

16	3	2	13
5	10	11	8
9	6	7	12
4	15	14	1

What is the magic number of this 5 x 5 magic square?

12	23	9	20	1
19	5	11	22	8
21	7	18	4	15
3	14	25	6	17
10	16	2	13	24

THE FIFTEENS GAME

This is a game for two players.
Use a set of cards numbered from 1 to 9. Draw a 3 x 3 grid on paper or card, large enough to fit a card into each square.

One player uses the odd-numbered cards, the other uses the even-numbered cards. Take turns to place a card in a square in the grid.

The winner is the first player to complete a line of three, horizontally, vertically or diagonally, which totals 15.

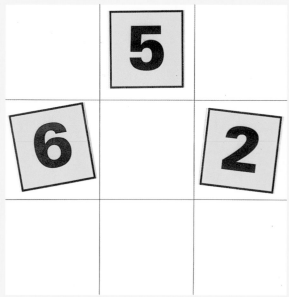

It is possible to create other magic shapes. This is a magic triangle. *Check that its magic number is 12.*

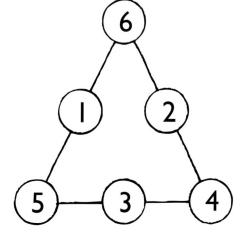

MAGIC TRIANGLES

Can you rearrange the numbers from 1 to 6 in this triangle to create a magic triangle with a magic number of 11? Now try for 10 and 9.

(15) MULTIPLYING

Some multiplications can be done with fingers and thumbs.

FINGER MULTIPLYING BY 9

Here is a trick for multiplying a number by 9. Hold out both hands with fingers and thumbs outstretched. Imagine that they are numbered as in the diagram.

To multiply 4 by 9, bend down finger 4.

Count the number of fingers and thumbs which are pointing either side of this. There are 3 on the left (this is the 'tens'), and 6 on the right (this is the 'units').
So the answer is 36.

Try using this method to multiply 7 by 9, and 3 by 9.

MULTIPLYING BY 11

There is a trick which makes multiplying by 11 easy.
Look at these:

$$17 \times 11 = 187$$
$$23 \times 11 = 253$$
$$35 \times 11 = 385$$
$$42 \times 11 = 462$$

Use a calculator to try some more multiplications by 11.
Can you spot any pattern?

MORE FINGER MULTIPLYING

Here is another trick for using the fingers and thumbs to multiply. Hold out both hands with fingers and thumbs outstretched again. Imagine that they are numbered as in the diagram.

To multiply 7 by 8, touch together finger 7 and finger 8. Count the number of fingers and thumbs which are touching and below. There are 5 (this is the 'tens').

Count the number which are above on each hand. There are 3 and 2. Multiply them together: 3 x 2 = 6 (this is the 'units'). So the answer is 56.

Try using this trick to multiply 8 by 6, 9 by 7, and 8 by 8.

CALCULATORS

Some calculator digits can look like letters of the alphabet when turned upside down.

If a large number is keyed into the calculator, which is then turned upside down, it is possible to create a word.

Turn this page upside down to read the word on the calculator display.

CALCULATOR CHALLENGE

Use your calculator to make some words of your own.

CALCULATOR STORIES

Here is a calculator story for you to translate:

This is a story about _ _ _ _   4121 + 1542
which are surrounded by _ _ _ _ _ _   115469 x 5
They come in different _ _ _ _ _ _   5 x 10643
I prefer the _ _ _ ones   103 x 6
You can eat them raw or you can _ _ _ _ them,   1777 x 4
but many people fry them in _ _ _.   10 x 71

Create your own calculator story.

BACK TO THE START

Here are two tricks with a calculator. Check the calculations using your calculator.

Choose a three-digit number, say 568 568
Repeat the digits to make a six-digit number 568568
Divide by 13 43736
(it divides exactly!)
Divide by 11 3976
(it divides exactly again!)
Divide by 7 568
(it divides exactly yet again!)

Notice that the result is the same three-digit number we started with. *Try this with other three-digit numbers. Do you always finish up with the number you started with?*

Choose any two-digit number, say 73 73
Repeat the digits with zero in between 73073
Divide by 13 5621
(it divides exactly!)
Divide by 11 511
(it divides exactly again!)
Divide by 7 73
(it divides exactly yet again!)

Again the result is the same three-digit number we started with. *Does this always work?*

FIND THE NUMBERS

Try these three calculator tricks on a friend

- Write down any number less than 10.
- Multiply by 7.
- Multiply by 16.
- Subtract the chosen number.
- Divide by 3.
- Divide by 37.

1

- Write down any number less than 10.
- Multiply by 5291.
- Multiply by 21.

2

- Write down any 2 two-digit numbers.
- Multiply one of them by 5.
- Add 36.
- Multiply by 20.
- Add the other two-digit number.
- Subtract 720.

3

17 SOLITAIRE

Solitaire is a game which was invented by a Frenchman in the eighteenth century, while he was in prison.

It is a one-person game.

The board has 33 holes. 32 pieces are placed, one in each of the holes except for the centre hole.

A move consists of jumping one piece over one other to an empty hole beyond. The piece which has been jumped over is removed. Moves can only be horizontal or vertical, not diagonal.

The object is to continue jumping and removing pieces until you have just one piece left.

The perfect finish is for this one last piece to be in the centre of the board.

There are a lot of variations of the game, based on using different-shaped boards and different numbers of pieces.

This game of Solitaire is played on a board shaped like a **pentagram**.

The rules are the same, and the objective is to finish up with just one counter left.

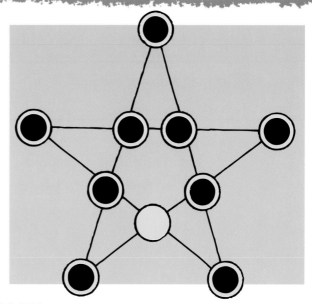

PENTAGRAM CHALLENGE

Can you do it?
Try on this board using counters.

This is a variation of the Solitaire game which includes scoring. The board is triangular.

Start by placing nine counters on any of these ten spots, leaving one clear.

Jump one counter over another, removing the jumped counter in the usual way.

Continue jumping and removing counters until you can jump no more, then add up the numbers on the empty spots. This is your score.

TO DO:

Play several games to see what is your best score.

GAMES WITH LINES

There are many games in which the aim is to complete a straight line of pieces. In some games, you have to try not to make a straight line.

This drawing shows that it is possible to place six counters on this 3 x 3 grid without completing a straight line of three counters.

CHALLENGE:

Place counters on this 4 x 4 grid. What is the highest number of counters you can place without having three counters in any one straight line?

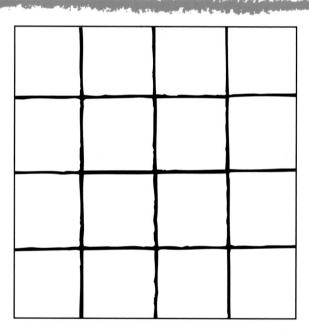

THREE-IN-A-LINE

This is a game for two players.
You need some counters each, of your own colour.
Take turns to place a counter on the 4 x 4 grid.
Game 1. The first player to have three of their counters in a straight line loses.
Game 2. The first player to have three of their counters in a straight line wins.

38

Another well-known game in which you aim to complete a straight line is the game of 'Noughts and Crosses'. This game is sometimes called 'Tic-Tac-Toe'.

In this game, you start by drawing two pairs of crossed lines, to give nine spaces. Two players ('O' and 'X') take turns to write their mark in one of the nine spaces. The winner is the player who first completes a straight line of three marks.

X		O
O	X	O
X		X

'x' wins

X	O	X
X	X	
O	O	O

'o' wins

NOUGHTS AND CROSSES

Play the game of 'Noughts and Crosses' with a friend. Then try these three variations of the game.

Variation 1. The first to get three in a line loses.

Variation 2. On your turn you may place your mark in as many spaces as you like, provided that they are all in the same straight line. They do not have to be next to each other. The player who makes the last mark or marks wins.

Variation 3. Play on a 4 x 4 grid. The first player to make a straight line of three in any direction wins.

THREE-DIMENSIONAL NOUGHTS AND CROSSES

A much more difficult variation of the game is to play it in three dimensions. Players place coloured marbles, instead of marking Os and Xs. There are 27 different positions in this game. The aim is still to make a straight line of three marbles, but they can be in any direction, horizontally, vertically or diagonally, and on any level.

FROGS

'Frogs' is one of many games and puzzles which are based on swapping the positions of two sets of pieces. The aim is to swap the positions of three male frogs and three female frogs.

You can try to solve the puzzle using three boys, three girls and seven chairs. Alternatively, you can use three counters of one colour to represent the female frogs and three counters of another colour to represent the male frogs. Then place them on a board like this so that the circles represent lilypads in a pond.

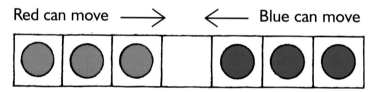

Red can move ⟶   ⟵ Blue can move

There are two ways that a frog can move:
- *Either* slide one space to an empty lilypad, in the direction shown.
- *Or* jump over one frog of the opposite sex to an empty pad beyond.

FROGS CHALLENGE 1

It is possible to swap the positions of the two sets of frogs in 15 moves. Can you do it?

FROGS CHALLENGE 2

Make a nine-lilypad pond with four male frogs and four female frogs. Can you solve this game of 'Frogs'?

COUNTER CHALLENGE

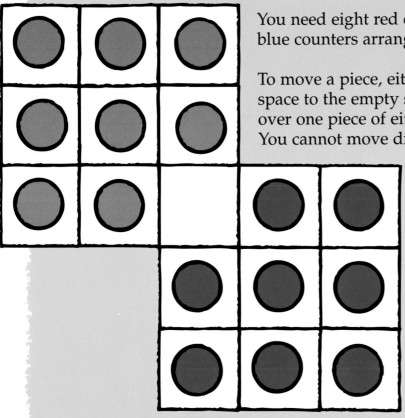

You need eight red counters and eight blue counters arranged like this.

To move a piece, either slide it one space to the empty square, or jump over one piece of either colour. You cannot move diagonally.

Can you change the positions of the red and blue counters?

SWAPPING PUZZLES

In each of these swapping position puzzles, you may only slide pieces horizontally or vertically – no jumping is allowed.
Can you solve the first puzzle in 16 moves and the second in 24 moves?

CHINESE TANGRAM

The tangram is an ancient Chinese puzzle. It resembles the familiar jig-saw puzzle, in that it is concerned with fitting together a set of shapes. There are seven pieces altogether, which can be cut from a square.

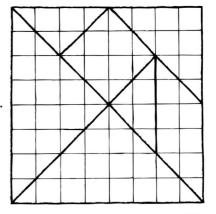

MAKE A TANGRAM

Make your own Chinese tangram by drawing the outline on some squared paper.

TANGRAM PICTURES

All of these pictures have been made by arranging the seven pieces. Try to make them.

In this picture 'Away in a Manger', each part is made from the same separate tangram. Create your own picture from tangrams.

Notice the shape of each of the tangram pieces. There is one square, one **parallelogram** and five **right-angled, isosceles triangles** (two small, one medium-sized and two large).

As well as arranging the pieces to create pictures, they can be arranged to make geometrical shapes. For example, this shows how to arrange them to make a rectangle.

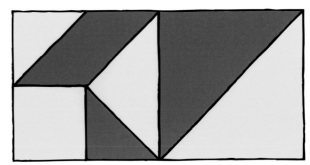

TANGRAM SHAPES

Can you arrange the seven tangram pieces above to make:
• a parallelogram
• a **trapezium**
• a right-angled triangle?

TANGRAM PUZZLE

Make this 3-piece tangram puzzle by drawing a square on card.
Mark the mid-points 1 and 2.
Use these as guides to draw the two lines.
Cut along the two lines to make three pieces.
Label them A, B and C.

Use the three pieces to see how many of these you can make:
• a triangle using A and B
• a triangle using A, B and C
• a rectangle using A, B and C
• a trapezium using A and B
• a trapezium using A and C
• a trapezium using B and C
• a trapezium using A, B and C
• a **pentagon** using A, B and C.

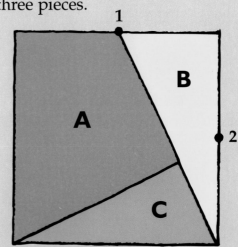

GLOSSARY

diagonal   A line drawn from one corner to an opposite corner.

horizontal lines   Straight lines drawn from left to right on the paper.

isosceles triangle   A triangle which has two equal sides.

magic number   The total of the rows, columns and diagonals in a magic square.

magic square   A square grid of numbers in which all rows, columns and diagonals have the same total.

multiple   The results of a multiplication table.

palindromic number   A number which reads the same forwards as backwards.

parallelogram   A quadrilateral with two pairs of parallel sides.

pentagon   A polygon with five sides.

pentagram   A shape made by joining the diagonals of a regular pentagon.

right-angled triangle   A triangle which has one right angle.

symmetrical pattern   Patterns are symmetrical when they have two matching halves, one a reflection of the other.

trapezium   A quadrilateral with one pair of parallel sides.

vertical lines   Straight lines drawn from the top to bottom, at right angles to a horizontal line.

INDEX

ANSWERS

p7

Coin sharing

50p, 20p, 20p, 10p and 50p, 20p, 10p, 10p, 5p, 5p

50p, 20p, 10p, 10p, 10p, and 50p, 20p, 20p, 5p, 5p

50p, 50p and 20p, 20p, 20p, 10p, 10p, 10p, 5p, 5p

p8

Straw squares

Straw division

p9

Straw equations

p10

Triplets

2,3,7; 6,5,1; 6,4,2; 7,4,1; 8,3,1; 9,2,1; 5,4,3.
6,5,4; 6,7,2; 6,8,1; 4,8,3; 4,9,2; 4,10,1; 5,8,2;
5,9,1; 5,7,3; 10,3,2.

p11

Sixteen card puzzle

One possible set of solutions is:

p12

Missing spots

p13   **Impossible dice**

p19   **Number maze**
Total of 15: pathway +6, +3, +5, +1
Largest total, 18; smallest total, 13
Different totals: 13, 14, 15, 16, 17, 18

p26   **Palindromic numbers are:**
101, 111, 121, 131, 141, 151, 161, 171, 181, 191
202, 212, 222, 232, 242, 252, 262, 272, 282, 292
303, 313, 323, 333, 343, 353, 363, 373, 383, 393

p30   **Magic number - 65**